A Mother's Journey

SANDRA MARKLE

ILLUSTRATED BY ALAN MARKS

ioi Charlesbridge

With love for my children, Scott and Holly—S. M.

To Carlos and Maria, my penguins—A. M.

Acknowledgments
Sandra Markle would like to thank the National Science Foundation for making it possible for her to explore Antarctica and observe its amazing wildlife in action. She would also like to thank Dr. Gerald Kooyman, professor emeritus at Scripps Institution of Oceanography, specializing in the diving behavior of emperor penguins; Dr. Barbara Wienecke and Dr. Graham Robertson, seabird ecologists with the Australian Antarctic Division, specializing in the winter behavior of female emperor penguins; and Dr. Roger Kirkwood, seabird ecologist with the Phillip Island Nature Park, Cowes, Victoria, specializing in the winter behavior of female emperor penguins, for sharing their expertise and enthusiasm. A very special thank you to Skip Jeffery for sharing the creative process and her life.

First paperback edition 2006

Published by Charlesbridge
85 Main Street
Watertown, MA 02472
(617) 926-0329
www.charlesbridge.com

Library of Congress Cataloging-in-Publication Data
Markle, Sandra.
  A mother's journey / Sandra Markle ; illustrated by Alan Marks.
    p. cm.
  ISBN 978-1-57091-621-2 (reinforced for library use)
  ISBN 978-1-57091-622-9 (softcover)
  ISBN 978-1-60734-068-3 (ebook pdf)
  1. Emperor penguin—Behavior—Juvenile literature. 2. Emperor penguin—Food—Juvenile literature. 3. Parental behavior in animals—Juvenile literature. I. Marks, Alan, 1957– ill. II. Title.
QL696.S473M36 2005
598.47—dc22   2004018954

Printed in Korea
(hc) 10 9 8 7 6 5 4
(sc) 10 9 8 7 6 5

Illustrations done in watercolor and ink
Display type and text type set in Caslon and Centaur
Color separated by Imago
Printed by Sung In Printing in Gunpo-Si, Kyonggi-Do, Korea
Production supervision by Brian G. Walker
Designed by Susan Mallory Sherman

In the rosy glow of the setting sun,

in mid-May, when Antarctica's winter has just begun,
a young female emperor penguin pushes out her egg.
It is the very first egg she has ever laid.

Cream white and cone shaped, it is softball sized
and steaming from her body's heat.
Her mate waddles fast to pick it up.
But bending forward,
she scoops the egg onto her feet.
Then she covers it with her belly flap
and holds it snug in her warm brood pouch.

The male sings his song and nudges her neck
until, at last, she lets the egg roll out.
This time the male scoops it up
and pushes it into his own brood pouch.
His winter's job has now begun.

During the next two months,
a tiny chick will grow inside the egg.
And all the while the male will
keep it warm and safe
from the fierce winter storms
that blow across the Antarctic ice.

The partners sing a last duet.

Then the young female joins
a line of female emperors
marching away from the colony.
She too has a job to do.

She needs to feed herself
and build up strength to be a mother.
Then shortly after the chick hatches,
she will come back with food
for her hungry baby.
But the closest food is in the open sea,
more than 50 miles away.

Flopping on her belly,
the young female scoots along,
following the others over the ice-crusted snow.
And the tracks they leave
trail after them.

50 miles is 80 kilometers

But the ice they are crossing
is just an ice sheet,
floating
on the sea.
So here and there the females
pop in to swim across the cracks.

When they come to
an iceberg,
gleaming and pointy,
the young female and the others
stand up and waddle through
the maze of scattered ice boulders.

On the second day a fiery green aurora
lights up the winter sky.
Then the plodding line of emperors
seems to dance,
with round black shadow partners
mimicking their steps.

On and on the young female travels
until, on the third day, the roaring wind
blows too hard to push through
and swirls diamond-dust snow
into a stinging cloud.
Then she joins the group,
standing close together.
With feathered backs out
and heads pulled in,
they huddle
to wait out the storm.

Day after day—five days in all—
the young female
and the other emperors plod and scoot
across the sea ice.
Then, finally, they reach the pack ice,
a patchwork quilt of milk-white chunks
stitched together by seams of blue-black water.

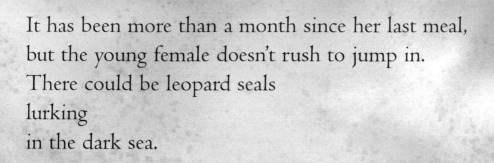

It has been more than a month since her last meal,
but the young female doesn't rush to jump in.
There could be leopard seals
lurking
in the dark sea.

The female emperors crowd together
at the very edge of the water.
Finally, those at the front dive in.
The others rush in after them.

Flapping her flippers,
the young female flies through the water,
zipping
this way and that,
until with swift and graceful twists
she swims into a school of shimmering silver fish
and easily
swallows her fill.

Every day, the young female searches for food—
sometimes alone and sometimes with others.
She always goes hunting when the sky is brightest,
even when that means hunting by moonlight.
She needs to see cracks in the ice cover
where she can poke her head out
and take a breath before diving again.

Some days, the young female dines on pink krill
plucked from clusters as thick as clouds.

Other days, she chases
fish and little squid
and, darting after them,
she gulps down all she can catch.

When she has no luck near the surface,
the young female dives deep down
through the dark, ice-cold water
to the bottom of the sea.
There, she nearly always catches
a scaly Antarctic jonasfish—
sometimes two or three.

One day a big leopard seal surprises her,
swimming up fast
from the dark depths
with its jaws open wide.
The young female pumps her flippers hard,
and, leaping in and out of the waves,
swims fast
and escapes.

Day after day, the young female hunts
and watches out for hunters.
In all, she travels
more than 930 miles.
But it is a zig-zag course
that never takes her too far
from the ice edge.

Then, one day, at the beginning of August,
as the ruby red sun
peeks
above the horizon,
the young female leaves the sea.
A feeling deep inside
tells her it is time to go.
If all is well, by now
her egg has hatched.

930 miles is 1,500 kilometers

The young female joins the other female emperors
heading back to the colony.
This time
they have even farther to go.
The area of ice they must cross has grown bigger
during the cold, dark winter months.
So, scooting and walking,
the little group hurries.
They have a long way to travel,
and the clock is ticking.

The newly hatched chicks
need the food
the females are bringing
stored in their bellies.
And their mates cannot wait
much longer to leave for the sea
to feed themselves.

For seven days
the female emperors march
through long, dark nights
and short, pale days,
through gusting winds
and blowing snow.

At last, ahead, they see the huddled mass
of waiting males.
Waddling into this group,
the young female sings
and listens hard
for just one singer
among all of the others.
Finally, she finds her mate.

Standing close, the pair bow their heads
and sing together.
Then the male rolls back his belly flap
and shows the young female
her very first chick.

At the sight of its mother,
the chick peeps to be fed.
And when the chick is settled on her feet,
she brings food up
and lets it eat.
With one last song,
her mate heads off to sea.
It is the young female's turn
to care for the little emperor.

But then that is exactly the reason
the new mother
has made her long journey.

Emperors Are Amazing!

Emperor penguins are the largest and heaviest kind of penguin, standing up to 44 inches (112 centimeters) tall and weighing as much as 90 pounds (41 kilograms).

- At sea, emperor penguins can dive deeper than any other bird. By attaching special depth recorders, scientists discovered emperors could dive down more than 1,600 feet (500 meters).
- Emperor penguins are the only animals that breed during the Antarctic winter.
- It only takes about 150 days from hatching for emperor chicks to reach maturity, when they're ready to be on their own.
- Like all penguins, an emperor penguin's bones are heavier than those of a flying bird. This helps them dive easily when they search for food.

Books:

Guiberson, Brenda Z. *The Emperor Lays an Egg*. New York: Henry Holt and Company, 2001. Details the chick's life cycle from the time it hatches until it's on its own.

Jenkins, Martin. *The Emperor's Egg*. Cambridge, MA: Candlewick Press, 1999. Focuses on the male penguin's two-month-long ordeal while incubating the egg during the harsh Antarctic winter.

Swan, Erin Pembrey. *Penguins: From Emperors to Macaronis*. New York: Franklin Watts, 2003. Explore how emperor penguins are like other kinds of penguins and how they are different.

Tatham, Betty. *Penguin Chick*. New York: HarperCollins Juvenile Books, 2002. Follow one emperor penguin chick and discover how it behaves and changes as it grows up.

Websites:

Creature Feature: Emperor Penguins
http://www.nationalgeographic.com/kids/creature_feature/0101/penguins.html
Discover fun facts about emperor penguins, see a map of where to find them, hear their voices, and more.

Mawson Emperor Penguins
http://www-old.aad.gov.au/science/AntarcticResearch/AMLR/aptenodytes/default.asp
Researchers at the Australian Antarctic Division have a long-running study of the Mawson breeding colony of emperor penguins. See pictures of the penguins and investigate these amazing birds with the scientists.

Author's Note:

Thanks to the U.S. National Science Foundation, I had the opportunity to explore Antarctica and its wildlife during two summers and one winter. Antarctica is an amazing place anytime, but the winter is truly awesome. Although the sun never rises for about four months, the moon in its phases never sets. Instead, the moon circles in the sapphire blue, star-studded sky, making the frozen world luminous. Sometimes an incredible light show, the aurora, casts an alien green glow. But beyond all the beauty, it's the cold and the wind that I remember most. The cold is painful and piercing. I had to wear layers upon layers of protective gear, including goggles to keep my contacts from freezing instantly to my eyes between blinks. Then there was the wind! It was sometimes so strong I could lean into it and not fall. And it blew the tiny, diamond-dust snowflakes into a swirling, blinding cloud. It was experiencing this fiercest of all winters on Earth firsthand that made me think what an incredible effort female emperor penguins make. Sure, credit is due to the males for sitting and incubating their eggs during the winter. But the females can't just hunker down and endure. They have to travel, find their way over an ever-changing landscape in the dark, find food, survive, and return. And they have to do all this in time to arrive shortly after their chick hatches. Female emperor penguins face an incredible challenge. This book honors their effort and applauds the fact that most succeed.